DUDLEY SCHOOLS
LIBRARY SERVICE

KU-349-745

Schools Library and Information Services

S00000782503

Muslim
Imam

Akbar Dad Khan

Photographs by Chris Fairclough

W

FRANKLIN WATTS
LONDON • SYDNEY

This edition 2009

Franklin Watts
338 Euston Road
London NW1 3BH

Franklin Watts Australia
Level 17/207 Kent Street
Sydney NSW 2000

Copyright © Franklin Watts 2001

ISBN 978 0 7496 8876 9

Dewey Decimal Classification Number 297

A CIP Catalogue record for this book is available from the
British Library

Series Editor: Ruth Nason
Design: Carole Binding

Reading Consultant: Lesley Clark, Reading and Language
Information Centre, University of Reading

The Author and Publishers thank Mr Masood Akhtar, his
assistants and the management committee of Luton
Central Mosque for their help in preparing this book.

The photograph on pages 18–19 is reproduced with the
permission of Corbis Images.

Printed in Malaysia

Franklin Watts is a division of Hachette Children's Books,
an Hachette Livre UK company. www.hachettelivre.co.uk

DUDLEY SCHOOLS LIBRARY SERVICE	
S00000782503	
£6.99	J297
10-Dec-2015	PETERS

Contents

Hello!

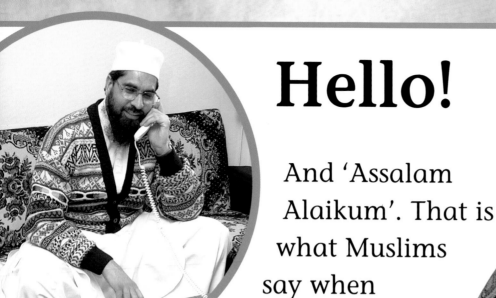

And 'Assalam Alaikum'. That is what Muslims say when they meet or telephone each other. It is Arabic and it means 'Allah's blessings be with you'.

I am Masood Akhtar, the Imam at Luton Central Mosque.

A mosque is a place where Muslims pray to Allah. Luton Central Mosque is the third largest mosque in Britain.

My main job as Imam is to lead all the prayers in the mosque.

Praying together

Muslims pray to Allah five times every day. The square clocks on our board show the prayer times. The times are spread from before sunrise to late evening.

Muslims pray wherever they are – at home, at work, at school. But it is best to say the prayers together at the mosque.

As we pray, we move in a special way. We kneel and touch the floor with our forehead to show that we submit to Allah. This means that we promise to obey Allah in everything we do.

We praise Allah and ask for Allah's forgiveness and blessings.

Wudu

Muslims get ready to say their prayers by washing in a special way called wudu.

We wash our hands, mouth, face, arms, head and feet three times with clean water.

The place where we pray must be clean, too, so we take off our shoes when we enter a mosque. I also use a prayer mat, both at the mosque and at home.

The Qur'an

After morning prayer in the mosque, I go home to my flat and read the Qur'an. This is the Muslim holy book. It is written in beautiful Arabic script.

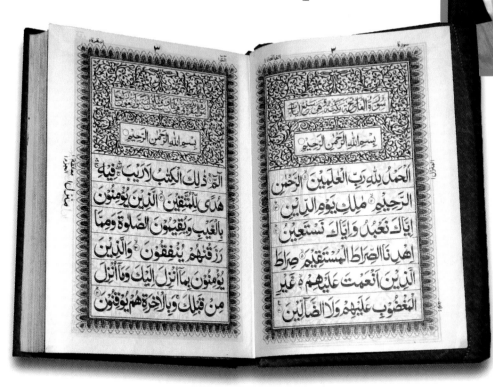

We handle the Qur'an with respect. When we read it, we rest it on a special stand, to keep it away from the floor.

Muslims believe that the words in the Qur'an are words from Allah, guiding people how to lead their lives. All Muslims learn some of the Qur'an by heart, to say as part of the five daily prayers.

Helping our community

I have breakfast and then I attend to phone calls and letters.

Many people in our community ask me for advice. I help them to think about what the Qur'an says and how it guides us in our everyday lives.

There is always lots to discuss with the people who look after the mosque. It is a big building, with two prayer halls, three classrooms, two washrooms and a library. It is open for a long time every day, for many different activities.

Explaining Islam

Many school parties visit our mosque. I show them around and explain what we do.

I show them our foundation stone.

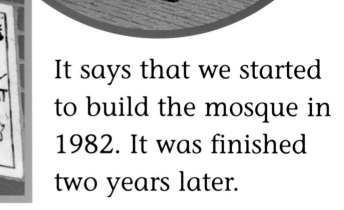

It says that we started to build the mosque in 1982. It was finished two years later.

On top of the minaret, there is a crescent moon. It is a symbol of our religion, Islam.

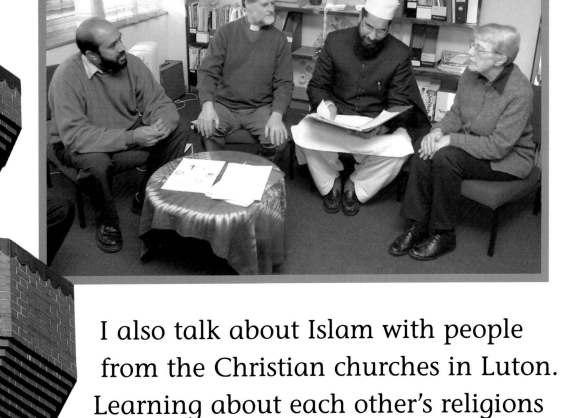

I also talk about Islam with people from the Christian churches in Luton. Learning about each other's religions helps us all to live together happily.

THERE IS NO DEITY ONLY ALLAH MUHAMMAD IS THE MESSENGER OF ALLAH

The Shahadah

The board on front of our mosque says what all Muslims believe. Allah is the only God (deity), and the Prophet Muhammad is the messenger of Allah. This sentence is called the Shahadah.

The Prophet Muhammad (peace be upon him) lived in Makkah, a city in Arabia.

He heard the Angel Gabriel give him Allah's message for all people. He recited what he heard and it was written down to form the Qur'an.

Each year Muslims from all over the world make a special journey to Makkah, called Hajj. When they get there, they go to the Grand Mosque and walk round the Ka'aba seven times. I hope I will go there one day.

Our prayer hall

The prayer hall in our mosque is decorated with patterns and Arabic writing. In the cupboard we keep copies of the Qur'an, wrapped in cloth as a sign of respect.

On the right in this picture is an alcove called the mihrab. It shows the direction of the Ka'aba in Makkah. All Muslims face towards the Ka'aba when they pray.

Here I am in front of the mihrab. Every day, before afternoon prayer, I give a talk about what the Qur'an teaches us.

Teaching

Children aged 6 to 15 come to the mosque every afternoon after school to learn the Qur'an.

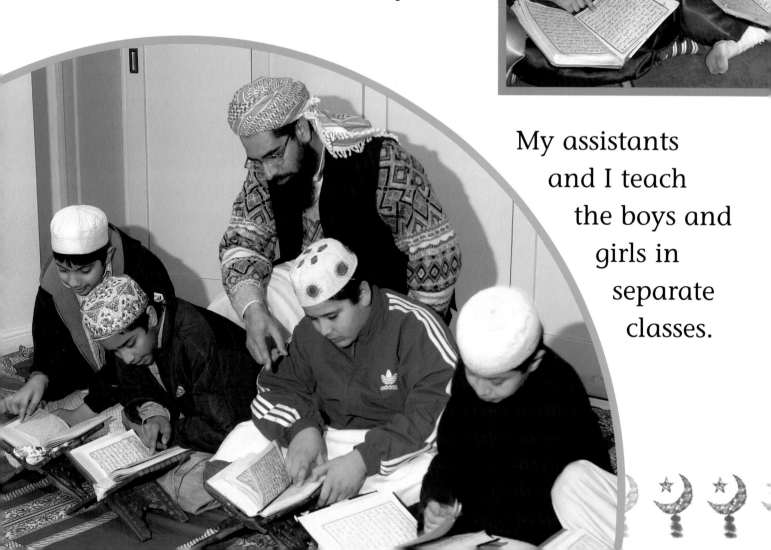

My assistants and I teach the boys and girls in separate classes.

We also teach the children to speak, read and write Urdu. Urdu is the language spoken by most of their parents and other relatives at home. Knowing Urdu helps the children to keep in touch with relations in Kashmir and Pakistan, too.

At weekends we run more activities for young people, like discussions and story-writing competitions.

Fridays

The Qur'an tells us that the afternoon prayer on Fridays is very important. Every week more than a thousand people come to our mosque for this prayer.

Before the prayer I give a lecture called khutba.

I study very hard to prepare my lecture, and I spend all of Friday morning getting ready for the afternoon prayer.

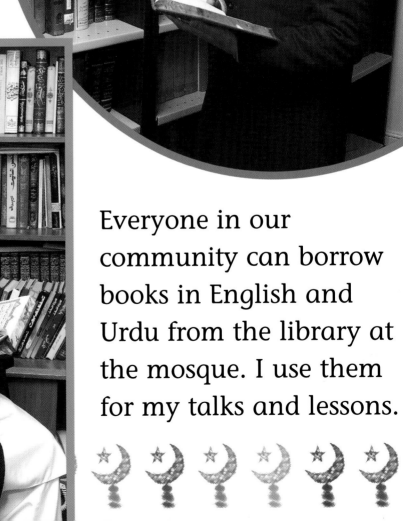

Everyone in our community can borrow books in English and Urdu from the library at the mosque. I use them for my talks and lessons.

Every Friday the mosque becomes a centre of activity for young and old. After the main afternoon prayers, people stay to pray in other ways. Some count prayer beads as they pray.

Small groups get together for more prayers, and there is a chance to talk and share ideas.

My work gives me great satisfaction. I feel glad to be serving our community as an Imam!

Glossary

Allah

The name that Muslims use for God. The most important Muslim belief is that Allah is the only God. Muslims worship only Allah. They must not make pictures of Allah.

Arabic

The language used by Muslims when they pray, and in which the Qur'an is written. It was the language spoken in Arabia, where the Prophet Muhammad started the first community of Muslims.

blessings

Feelings of deep happiness that Muslims believe can come from Allah.

community

A group of people who live close together or share beliefs or interests.

Hajj

A journey to Makkah, the holy city of Islam, where the Prophet Muhammad started the first Muslim community. It is a duty for Muslims to go on Hajj once in their life, if they can afford it.

holy

Connected with God.

Islam

The religion of Muslims. The word means obedience to Allah and also peace.

Ka'aba

A building in the centre of the Grand Mosque in Makkah. It has a special importance in Islam. Muslims everywhere face towards the Ka'aba when they pray.

minaret

A tall tower on a mosque. In the past, and in some places today, a Muslim called a muezzin called out from the tower to tell people when a prayer time was starting.

Prophet Muhammad

A prophet is someone that God has chosen to give people his message. Muslims believe that the Prophet Muhammad was the last and most important prophet. He lived in Arabia (now called Saudi Arabia) nearly 1500 years ago. Out of respect, Muslims always add 'peace be upon him' after speaking or writing his name.

recite

To say something that you have learned carefully by heart.

Shahadah

A sentence which sums up what Muslims believe. Saying the Shahadah is one of five things that Muslims must do. The others are: praying five times a day, giving money to the poor, fasting in the special month of Ramadan, and going on Hajj.

wudu

A special way of washing before prayer. All mosques have a place for wudu.

Index